Mastering You

Neville Goddard

Manifesting with Ease

By

Rita Faith

Text Copyright © 2016

All rights reserved

No part of this publication may be reproduced, stored in a retrieval system, or transmitted, in any form or by any means without the prior written permission of the author, nor be otherwise circulated in any form of binding or cover other than that in which it is published and without a similar condition being imposed on the subsequent purchaser.

Please note that much of this publication is based on personal experience and evidence. Although the author and publisher have made every reasonable attempt to achieve complete accuracy of the content in this book, they assume no responsibility for errors or omissions. Also, you should use this information as you see fit, and at your own risk. The suggestions found in this book are expressly the opinion of the author; following these suggestions is at the sole discretion and risk of the reader, who assumes full responsibility for his/her actions in relation to the information contained herein. Finally, nothing contained herein is intended to replace common sense, legal, medical or other professional advice, and is meant to inform and entertain the reader

Table of Contents

Introduction

Changing Mental States

How Revision Works

From Doubt to Faith

Feeling Is the True Power

True Meaning of Detachment

Manifesting with Ease

Thank You

Introduction

In this book I explain the teachings of Neville Goddard and break it down in a way that makes it easier for the reader to understand and implement the teachings in day to day life. The Book focuses on the art of changing mental states and dying to the old state; not in the physical sense but in the dying too undesirable states and teaches the reader how to use this in order to change the circumstances of life.

You will also learn how revision actually works and how you can put it to use to stop the circle of negative events and circumstances that you may be experiencing in your life. By using revision you will change your memory image and therefore change the undesirable to the desirable.

We then look at how to replace doubt with faith, how to feel it in and the true meaning of detachment. These chapters give you practical advice and understanding on these areas of manifesting, so that you manifest much more successfully. The book concludes with a chapter on manifesting with ease, in the hope that you will finally start to achieve your desires and do so without fear or frustration, but with simplicity and ease.

Becoming master of your inner world is to learn to become an affecter of your life. You will no longer be at the mercy of your physical senses but will become a powerful creator knowing that your imagination is the key to changing your outer world. Changing your inner world will result in corresponding changes in your outer; it is a universal law.

It is my desire that you will find my insights and further explanations on Neville's teachings and suggestions on actively putting it to use, so that it gives you a deeper understanding of the methods and principles involved in the successful use of your wonderful imagination to change your world.

We all have the same power and we can all experience this power by persistently and consistently operating it, so that we are not trapped in a reality that we do not wish to be in. There are many ways we can use our imagination to achieve this and this book explains these techniques in a way that you can actually grasp how to apply them in your day to day life.

There are many books on manifestation and law of attraction, but this book explains how to make it work using only the teachings of Neville Goddard, his teachings are the truth and are not watered down in any way. This book does not contain any information on affirmations or vibration. It is simple and concise and explains the powerful teachings of Neville.

I know through my own experience that if you fully apply the information contained within this book then you will change your reality and become the master of your World.

Changing Mental States

"In spite of all things round about you that deny it, you walk as though your wish were true. And in a way that you do not know, it will externalize itself within your world and you will actually receive it." – Neville Goddard

Neville taught that we have the power to realize our every dream, as God and man are one. The power that God gave us is our imagination, which is the only creative power in the universe. However in order to use this power effectively and consciously, it has to be operated, and as the individual we are the operant power of our own imagination.

Therefore the control and intensity of our imagination determines the events and circumstances we encounter in our life. Knowing this we must consciously guide our imagination, thoughts and feelings towards our dreams, that is imagining and entertaining feelings that suggest that our dreams are already a present fact.

In order to change states, you must learn to die to your current state. That is dying to your former mental state, dying to your perceived limitations, dying to fear and doubt, dying to the thoughts and feelings that are keeping you locked into your present reality.

In order to change your circumstances you must die to your former thoughts, feelings, fears, doubts and all sensory evidence that is contrary to that which you desire, and rise again in a new consciousness. For example die to the state of poverty by no longer focusing on lack and limitation, and rise to a new consciousness, that is the state of wealth and imagine wealth, spending money, being congratulated on your good fortune. Focus on the feelings of relief, security and contentment. Turn away from the physical senses and live in your imagination focusing on and feeling wealthy.

This is dying to one state and rising again in a new state. The problem many of us face is that we take a long time to do it or never rise again. What I mean is that we are so tied into the physical senses that we have formed the habit of only imagining, thinking and feeling what the senses dictate, or rather the "facts" of life, so that we never truly die to that state, which we must do in order to fully feel the new desired state, as in from the state of poverty to the state of wealth.

So if you don't die and turn away from the state of poverty, you will remain in that state and never experience the state of wealth.

You have the power to create any state you so desire, but you must die to the former state and rise to your ideal state and you do this by turning your back on the past and all current evidence of your physical senses. Rise in your imagination and feelings to a new desired state and it will manifest in your world!

You can daydream and want things to be different all day, every day. But if you don't die to your present state of mind and reactions to life nothing is going to change. You must die to your present state and then occupy and live in your new state, you do this by living in your imagination and feeling the reality of the desired state now, controlling your inner conversations and watching your reactions to life. If you don't do this then the new state cannot enter your outer world.

Have so much faith, belief and trust in the power of your imagination that you can completely die to your former beliefs, thoughts and feelings and evidence of your senses, ignore the present "facts", which are only the out picturing of your former state of mind. If you do this and do it consistently and persistently, by imagining, walking and living in your desired state, then, I promise you that your old circumstances will crumble and fade out of your reality and new circumstances will manifest.

Imagination is God and the Power that sustains the universe and is the Power, the only Power, which can set you free from any undesired circumstances in your current life. Nothing is impossible to God, and as your imagination is God, nothing is impossible to you. Believe in yourself!

What do you long for? What do you desire? How would you feel if you realized your desire? You can prophesy it for yourself, which is you can predict your future. How do you do it?

You know what you want, and then you single out an event, or an act, or a conversation that would imply the fulfilment of that desire. You then contemplate on that desire, which is you imagine in your mind, asking yourself all the time, how would I feel if it were true? Then you play the event, act or conversation over and over again in your imagination, which implies that your desire is realized. For example hearing a friend congratulate you, or celebrating with champagne, hearing the pop of the cork, the clinking of glasses as you toast your success.

You do this over and over until you get the feeling that satisfies, in other words, you fully feel how you would feel if your desire was a present fact. Feel the movement in your body, fully feel it until you feel contentment, relief or a feeling of satisfaction. Then carry that feeling with you like a fragrant odour in your waking life. Live in this feeling, this new state and completely die to your former state. You cannot long for that which you already have, so you die to the longing by persisting in the assumption that your desires are realized. You have so buried the former state that it can no longer be found.

While you are changing mental states, it is important that you don't start looking for signs that your desires are on the way, as this is a sure fire way to bring doubt and worry, and ultimately leads to creating what you don't want. You see in looking for signs, you are admitting that you don't have what you want yet, you are focusing on the lack of your desire. This leads to feelings of worry and frustration. This in turn creates more of the same.

You must learn to let go and detach from your present circumstances, detach from the feelings of lack and frustration. Learn to detach and be unaffected by the evidence of the senses. Think on and feel only the desired reality as if it were already true.

You may feel that this is madness or you are losing your grip on reality, but this is what you must do – Go Mad as in trust only in your imagination, knowing that what you are thinking and feeling will objectify itself, this is abandonment to the feeling of your desired state.

Don't accept into your consciousness anything that denies the fulfilment of your desire. Your imagination is the only reality; the outer world is simply the out picturing of your imagination, thoughts and feelings.

Surrender to the feelings of the wish fulfilled. Live in the desired reality in your imagination, and stay faithful to it. Die to your former state of mind – lift yourself up in consciousness. This is when miracles will happen.

Do you believe that your imagination is God? Do you believe that you have the same power to create as God has? Do you believe you are God? If God is all powerful, and you are God, then you are all powerful!

We have been given this amazing gift of imagination, to use our imagination to change and feel our way into any state. We are keyed low, that is there is a time lag between our imaginative acts and feelings and the subsequent manifestation on the physical plane.

However if we remain persistent and guide our thoughts and feeling to yield to the assumption that our desires are a present fact, they will and must manifest in our reality. This is God's promise. Crucify yourself to your desired state, so that nothing can disturb you. Ignore the evidence of the senses, and your desire will objectify itself, it is a universal law.

Believe the promise. Believe in your imagination. Believe in yourself!

We are all creatures of habit and we are all in the habit of doing and experiencing the same things. We find comfort in the habit of knowing that everything is the same, that it is fixed. Even if we don't like it, we are used to it, it is how things are, and it is facts.

However Neville taught there is another way that you can escape your current reality, no matter where you are. You can use your imagination to lift yourself up to a new state of consciousness, it may feel unnatural to do it, it may feel like you are going mad causing you to stay with what you think is reality and the evidence of the senses.

If you could ignore the senses and deny all evidence that is contrary to your desire and, go "mad" by abandoning yourself to the thoughts and feelings of your desired state, you will change your world. It may feel unnatural at first and you may fall back into the old thoughts and feelings, but if you persist and continue to bring your thoughts and feelings back to the fulfilled desire, it will become natural and your outer reality will change to reflect your new inner state. Then you will have died mentally to your former state and your dreams will become reality.

When I am saying go mad, I do not mean pretending to be a millionaire or that you run around and start telling people you are happily married, when you don't even have a partner in your current reality. What I mean is that you feel the feelings that your desire is manifest now. That you have inner conversations that imply that your reality is as you want it to be.

You turn your back on the evidence of the senses, so that you can imagine and fully feel what you would feel if your desire were a present fact. This going mad is not allowing your current experience to dictate your thoughts and feelings. You have the free will to choose what you will imagine, think and feel. Only allow what you want to experience into your consciousness. This is how you bring it forth into your physical world.

For example if you are single and desire a loving, happy relationship. Imagine in your mind you and your perfect partner, holding hands, laughing as you walk along in the sunshine. Feel the warmth of their skin in your hand, put your head on their shoulder, and bask in the feeling of love. Hear your laughter, as they tell you something funny. Hear them tell you that they love you. Abandon yourself to this feeling of love and contentment.

Keep your imagined scene short and simple and play it over and over in your head every day, but most importantly feel it. How would it feel if it were true? Allow yourself to be absorbed into those feelings, if you do this consistently and persistently, you will create that loving relationship. It will and must objectify in your outer reality. By feeling it in the inner, it must manifest in the outer. This is true of any mental state you allow yourself to become absorbed in, so only allow yourself to be absorbed into imaginings and feelings that you desire to manifest as circumstances and events in your life.

I implore you to test and experiment with your imagination. Neville knew as I also know that imagination creates reality. We have an extraordinary gift, but we have been so led to believe that we are unworthy or incapable of changing who we are or our circumstances, that we have become blind to the power of our imagination and have become victims to our physical senses.

I have personally experienced the power of my imagination and I know beyond a shadow of a doubt that Neville Goddard's teachings are true. The more you test and experiment with your imagination, you will discover the truth about who you are and how powerful your imagination is.

It is the power that can lift you to heights that you never thought you could experience, but you must consciously operate it. Your imagination also has the power to take you into the depths of despair if you allow it to be operated by the evidence of the senses. Whether you operate it consciously or unconsciously it is always creating your life.

The only price you have to pay to create your desire is to turn your back on the evidence of the senses and die to your former state of mind. You don't have to beg for it, you don't have to exhaust yourself working for it; you don't have to figure out how it can come to you. You don't have to be forgiven for any perceived wrongs you imagine you have done. All you have to do is completely abandon yourself to the feeling of your desired state, concentrate on the inner and the outer will conform to your change of mental state.

How Revision Works

"Now, this exercise calls for, I would say, the active, voluntary use of imagination as against the passive, involuntary acceptance of appearances. We never accept as true and as final anything unless it conforms to the ideal we desire to embody within our world. But now we start it and we do it daily. You may get your results tomorrow; it may come the day after; it may come in a week, but I assure you they will come." – Neville Goddard

The above Neville quote is from a lecture he gave explaining his technique of revision, which is to mentally change anything that has happened that you don't like and making it conform to how you wished it had happened. By changing the memory of the event you alter the past and that therefore alters your present and future experiences.

Revision is a powerful technique; the results from practicing revision consistently can be simply amazing. Neville went as far as saying that he believed there were no limitations to the power of this technique. Neville likened revision to forgiveness and stressed that this was true forgiveness as you are changing your memory to such an extent that you are forgetting anything or anyone that displeased you, and changing it to how you would like things to be thereby erasing from your memory negative events and circumstances and replacing the memory impression to conform to your ideal. This is what breaks the negative cycle of events and circumstances in your life.

At the end of each day while you are in bed, you mentally review your day and if there is anything in your day that did not go the way you would have wished it to go, mentally revise the scene to how you would have liked it to have played out and do it with such intensity and feeling that it becomes the new memory image and therefore replaces the actual memory of the day. For instance if you received a bill that upset you and you didn't have the money to pay it; mentally revise that scene and upon opening the bill, imagine yourself paying it straight away and feeling content and relief that you paid it as soon as you received it. Play the scene over and over again in your imagination until you get the feeling that satisfies, that feeling of relief that it is done. Then move on to the next scene, revising each scene that displeased you in any way. This could be revising an argument with someone into a pleasant conversation or rewriting mentally an upsetting email or letter to conform to your ideal. You can revise absolutely anything, but always do so until you get the feeling that satisfies, which makes it feel real in your imagination. Then as you fall asleep you are taking these new revised memory images into your consciousness, these go forth into your future experience; this is how you break the cycles of events and experiences in your life.

I always struggled getting up in the mornings and always felt tired and lethargic, often waking up late or snoozing my alarm until I had to jump out of bed and rush around, this led to me feeling stressed and annoyed every morning, as you can imagine this is not a good way to start the day!

I used revision successfully and within about one week I was waking up refreshed and full of energy and eager to start my day, often waking up before my alarm went off. All I did was imagine each and every night for around a week, when I went to bed that I had awakened that morning bright and early, feeling refreshed and full of energy. I imagined feeling calm and happy and how I loved being an early riser. Having changed my morning memory image with feeling in my imagination, it went forth and changed my reality, so that, what I had experienced in imagination objectified itself in my outer world.

"Don't blame; only resolve. It is not man or the earth at their loveliest, but you practicing the art of revision make paradise. The evidence of this truth can lie only in your own experience of it. Try revising the day. It is the pruning shears of revision that we owe our prime fruit" – Neville Goddard

It is not only events that happened that we can change through revision, but if there was something that you desired to happen that did not, then you can revise your day and add the event in as if it was an actual fact. For instance suppose you have been waiting to hear about a job interview, you would then imagine that you had just came out of that interview feeling confident and happy that it had went so well. This not only suggests that you had in fact been invited to an interview, but that you had already had the interview and it went amazingly well.

Also you can revise your day as you go, you don't have to wait until you go to bed to review your day, you can mentally change anything at any time throughout the day as long as you make sure that you get the feeling that satisfies and have self-persuaded yourself in the reality of your new revised scene. If you have just had a telephone conversation that didn't go well, revise it there and then, even keeping the telephone to your ear, after the call has ended, and mentally hear what you wished you had heard on the call. Then when you get the feeling that satisfies, put the phone down and forget about it and get on with your day. This stops you taking any negative conversation into your consciousness, thereby stopping its effect in your world.

Use revision and use it daily, the more you make this technique a part of your daily routine, the easier it becomes and you will find that you never accept as final anything that happens in your outer world. You change it to conform to your ideal, so you will stop dwelling and focusing of the negative, and truly begin to live in your imagination. This is when you break the cycles in your life, this is what Neville meant when he said that you will never again accept the facts of life, but live in your imagination and put everything in subjection to it. This is when you become a true master of your inner world; seeming miracles will begin to appear. But only to the degree that you practice and persist, as I have said so many times before, knowledge without action is only knowledge, it changes nothing. However applied and persistence use of this knowledge will change your world. It costs you absolutely nothing to try it, and it is only through trying it and I mean persistently that you experience the truth of it. Imagination is reality and you are the operant power.

From Doubt to Faith

"The word Satan means doubt. Desiring a certain state, reason may tell you it will be difficult to attain. If you listen to your reason and doubt your desires, Satan has made himself known to you" – Neville Goddard

Doubt the major obstacle that stops us from manifesting our desires on a consistent basis, is doubt. How can we rid ourselves of this obstacle? The answer is Faith. Doubt is the absence of faith, if we had complete faith then doubt could not live in our minds, the door would be closed and doubt would be left out in the cold where it belongs.

So what is faith? Faith is the assurance of the things we hope for and the conviction of things not yet seen. Your imagination is the power by which you can bring your desires into form but only to the degree of your faith in your imagination as the creative power in your life, this gives you an inner conviction that your desires will manifest. The only thing that can stop your manifestation is your lack of persistence in the feeling of your desired state and faith in your imagination which then allows doubt to take hold of you.

The way to go about removing doubt and fear from your mind is to detach yourself from the evidence of the senses and your reactions to it. Stop allowing yourself to be controlled by the outer world, the outer is only a reflection of your inner world. To rid yourself of doubt, deny the evidence of the senses, ignore anything that is in contrast to what you desire.

The minute doubt or anxious and fearful thoughts make an appearance in your mind, don't react to them. Turn away and bring your attention to what you desire, think on what you want in place of what you have. Fully focus on what you desire, contemplate it, feel it as if it were true now. Then you are consciously using your imagination and in the present you are creating your future. Turn your attention away from everything you don't want and focus on your desire, live in the end as if it has happened.

As my book on inner talking explained, you must put off your old conversations and put on the new conversations which suggest the reality of your desires already fulfilled. The old conversations were full of doubt and fear, the new conversations are full of knowing and contentment, there is no home for doubt when desires are already fulfilled, there is no longing, or what if's. There is relief, there is contentment, there is peace, and there is joy.   So where can doubt live?

A few years back, I needed money for an operation. I did not have the money and could think of no way that I could acquire the money. Knowing that my imagination was the power that created my reality, this is what I did.

Three times a day, in the morning, afternoon and when I went to bed at night I imagined that I was sitting up in my hospital bed being examined by the doctor after my operation. I heard him telling me that the operation was a success and that he was very happy with how I was doing. I heard myself tell him that I was so pleased that the operation was over and that I was feeling really good.

I felt the relief and contentment that everything had went as planned and that the operation was a success. I always imagined that scene, the end as in the operation having already been performed and successful. Throughout my waking days I would smile to myself and feel grateful that it was done and always the inner conversation I had with the Doctor and the image of him examining me after the operation came into my consciousness. This I did for around two weeks and then the money came to me for the operation, totally out of nowhere from a source I would never have thought possible.

By imagining the end only, the means to the realization of my desire came to me. This is the power we all possess. What I did not do, was try to figure out "how" I could get the money for the operation. I didn't even imagine getting the money for the operation, as by doing either of those doubts would have crept in. The money wasn't what I desired, what I desired was to have the operation and for it to be a success. I knew how I would feel if it were true so in my imagination and inner conversations I imagined the end and felt the feelings of my fulfilled desire. I died to the state of someone needing money for an operation and I rose to the state of someone who had just had a successful operation. Where was doubt? Doubt had no place in my mind as I saw and lived in the end in complete faith that it was done.

    Always go to the end, as if it has happened, do not focus on what needs to happen in order to get to the end, as this is where doubt sneaks in and it causes fearful thoughts and leads to frustration and a feeling of force. This only creates more frustration in your life; remember your feelings are powerful. Always notice what you are feeling and ask yourself, what is this feeling creating right now? If you don't like what your current feeling will manifest if you persist in it, then change your thoughts and inner conversation and die to that state. Lift yourself up in consciousness, think on your desire, commit yourself to the feeling of it, give it all of your attention and focus; love it completely. If you persist in this, doubt, fear and any anxious thoughts will lose their power and die, they will disappear from the mind and be replaced by an inner conviction; they will be replaced by Faith! Try it you have nothing to lose, but doubt and fear!

Feeling Is the True Power

"What you feel deeply is far more important than what you are thinking. You may think about doing something for a long time and never do it, but when you feel something deeply you are spurred to act – and God acts! He who is the cause of all life acts through the sense of feeling. You can think of a thousand things, yet not be moved to act upon one of them. A deep conviction – felt, is far more important than anything you could ever think." – Neville Goddard

Neville always emphasised the importance of feeling above everything else, he even wrote the book, feeling is the secret, so as to highlight the importance of feeling your desires to become reality, where there is no feeling, there is no power. This is the difference between idle daydreaming and manifesting your desires again and again.

Through the use of feeling the fulfilment of your desire, you are feeding that state and it will become reality. If however you only think about your desire as some hope of it being true in the future, you are feeding your hunger for it and it will continue to evade you. Feeling anything deeply will move you to act on that feeling. You must feed the desire with the persistent assumption that it is true and the only way you can do that is through the act of feeling, the true power lies in the depth of your feeling that it is true.

Feeling is like faith, to have true faith you must act on the conviction that what you want is already yours, and the only way to do that is through the power of feeling. How would you feel if you were wealthy? What would the feeling be like? Identify the feeling and live in that feeling, morning, noon and night. Do not let anything disturb your state.

If you feel wealthy, you will see opportunities to make money and act on these opportunities, wealth will be drawn to, regardless of anything that is happening on the outside, or what state the economy is in, if you feel deeply enough that you are wealthy and persist in that feeling, boundless opportunities will come your way and you will always be wealthy, as you are living in the state of wealth.

You may be wondering, how exactly do you feel as if you are wealthy, when in your current reality you are not wealthy? How can you feel an abundance of money when you have never had an abundance of money and are always struggling?

This all comes down to your imagination and changing your focus and attention. Imagine how you would feel if you were wealthy, what would the feeling be like if you had all the money you needed to enjoy a life of freedom, security and peace of mind? What does having an abundance of money mean to you? What would you be able to do? How would it affect your life? How would others see you? Ask yourself how would I feel if I were wealthy?

In your imagination, picture your life filled with money, imagine all the things you would do with this money. Imagine that your bank account is filled with money that you can buy whatever you want, you can pay all your bills on time easily and effortlessly. Think about how this will affect your family life. Imagine all the people in your family you could help, think about how you will feel when you are able to give easily and generously to your family.

What is the feeling you get when you are picturing this and imagining it in your mind? Are you feeling joy, happiness, inner peace, gratitude, relief? Identify the feeling regarding what having an abundance of money would mean to you. It is this feeling that you have to ignite within you. Then relax and get into a sleepy state with your eyes closed, feel this exact feeling, be absorbed by this feeling and then single out an event, or conversation that you believe you would encounter following the fulfilment of your desire. For example, depositing a cheque into your bank account, celebrating with friends or being congratulated. Then play this scene over and over in your imagination while feeling the feelings that it has already happened. When you come out of your session go about your day but remain faithful to your imaginative act. That is do not entertain feelings of poverty, lack or struggle but persist in the feeling of your imaginative act and ignore anything that suggests otherwise.

The essence of money is freedom, security, peace of mind. This is what you should be focusing on and when you consciously guide your attention and thoughts toward this, you will ignite the feelings of joy, happiness, inner peace, relief, contentment and gratitude. You have to stop worrying and focusing on lack, by feeling as if you are already financially abundant now in the present moment. You think from your desire by feeling that it is already a present fact, rather than thinking of your desire which is wishing that it would happen. This is the difference between success and failure.

When you are worrying about money, you are placing your attention on lack and struggle. You are then igniting feelings of fear, despair and frustration. This only serves to keep you locked into your reality of lack and struggling. What does worrying lead you too? Is it helping you in any way?

Worrying only aids in attracting to you more thoughts of a similar nature, your mind will go on a rampage of worry, your thoughts will be fear based, full of doubt in the power of your imagination, full of negative scenarios. What you are actually doing is using your imagination to create lack and frustration. Your imagination is always creating your reality; this is true whether it is good, bad or indifferent.

You must have faith; worry is the opposite of faith. To become a conscious operator of your wonderful imagination you must have faith that your imagination is the only creative power in the universe.   You have an inner conviction that whatever you are imagining with feeling, and remain faithful to, will objectify itself in your outer world.

Have that inner knowing, that despite any outside sensory evidence to the contrary that your imaginative acts and feelings are going forward into the future and will manifest in your outer world. That it is already a present fact, it has happened in imagination so it is already real. This is faith, this is belief, and this is knowing without a shadow of a doubt that your imagination is the creator of your life experiences and circumstances.

What would the feeling be like if it were true? What conversations would you be having with friends and family if you already had your desire? What would you see? What would others be saying about your news? Answer these questions, by imagining in your mind the fulfilment of your desire, ignite your feelings, take note of them and continue to ignite these very feelings daily and you will be feeling the reality of your desire now, as if it was a present fact. Surrender yourself to those feelings, delight in them, be absorbed by them and in a way you do not know your outer world will change to reflect your new inner state.

True Meaning of Detachment

"We must practice separating ourselves from our negative moods and thoughts in the midst of all troubles and disasters of daily life. No one can be different from what he is now unless he begins to separate himself from his present reactions and to identify himself with his aim. Detachment from negative states and assumption of the wish fulfilled must be practiced in the midst of all blessings and cursing of life" – Neville Goddard

If you have been studying Law of Attraction or Neville or any other metaphysical teacher, you will have heard the importance of detaching or letting go. There is a lot of confusion out there on what this actually is. A lot of people assume that they have to stop thinking about what they want in order for it to manifest, this is not what Neville taught. If you stop thinking about and feeling what you desire how will it ever manifest? The true meaning of detachment is to detach yourself from your present circumstances and reactions to it, no matter what is going on.

Neville taught that you had to detach from your present circumstances and the "facts" of your current life. Notice the difference here? He taught that you must detach from all sensory evidence which denied the fulfilment of your desire, ignore it! This is the true meaning of detachment, it is not that you stop imagining, thinking and feeling what you desire, but rather detach from your present circumstances, negative moods and reactions to it, and live in the feeling of your wish fulfilled.

The importance of this is that whatever you are feeling and giving your focus to, you are giving energy too, you are creating your reality through your focus, attention and feeling at this very moment, so if you are using your imagination and focusing on thoughts, inner conversations and feelings that are being dictated by your current outer experience, you are effectively creating more of the same. These thoughts and feelings do not recede into the past but go forth and you will live them in your future. That is your world will not change as you are creating the same circumstances over and over by allowing them into your consciousness.

Even by reliving unpleasant experiences from the past and reliving the feelings you felt then, whether it is anger, guilt, fear, depression, unhappiness, what you are doing is using your imagination to create more of these types of experiences in your future. To resolve this use revision to change anything that didn't please you in your past experience, this way you are changing the impression of that event in your mind and in so doing you are creating a new mental impression, this then stops the past experience from continuing to create similar experiences and sets you free from the effects of those unpleasant events.

Detach from them and only imagine and feel the state you wish to manifest. Die to the former states and rise in consciousness to the state desired.

It is total abandonment to the feelings of your desire, complete faith that it will manifest. Detaching yourself from all the so called "facts" of life and allow yourself to be absorbed into the state you wish to see objectified in your outer world. Watch your reactions to life, if you are still reacting based on how things currently are then you are not detaching from your current state.

You must learn to ignore the evidence of the senses and persist in the assumption that your desires are a reality now. Use your inner conversations, revision and most importantly your feeling of the wish fulfilled to yield yourself to your new desired state. Persist, persist, persist! If you can master detachment to your present circumstances and your reactions to it, it will fade away and be replaced by your new state, which is your assumptions though at this moment false, will harden into fact. Your subjective world will and must objectify itself. Then you will discover just how powerful your wonderful human imagination is!

Manifesting with Ease

"When I speak of feeling, I don't mean emotion, but acceptance of the fact that the desire is fulfilled. And you can think you did that, but you can know for sure, if you don't have acceptance. And the reason you don't have acceptance is that you are still thinking OF the goal, rather than thinking FROM the goal" – Neville Goddard

If you have been trying unsuccessfully to manifest your desires, the causes are usually too much effort, lack of faith and or feeling and non-acceptance of your desired state, which is thinking OF your desire and not thinking FROM your desire as an accomplished fact.

When you apply too much effort, you are trying to force change and ultimately this leads to a feeling of frustration, it is this feeling of frustration that manifests and not what you desire to manifest. The feeling will always manifest regardless of what you are thinking, this usually happens by focusing on the "how" and not living in the end as if it has already happened. This is non-acceptance of the state desired.

Acceptance of the desired state is thinking from the desire, as in feeling its reality now. This is the feeling you must live in, morning, noon and night, this is what ensures its manifestation in your physical world. If you are only thinking of the desire it will not work, thinking of the desire only continues to keep it away from you, even if you are thinking about it every day, for years, it will not manifest. However the moment you begin to think from the desire, you start to call it forth and it will and must objectify itself, you have successfully imagined it happening now in your imagination with feeling and carried that feeling with you throughout your waking day. Every time you think of your desire, you think from it as if it has already happened and feeling the feelings of its reality in your world. As I described in how I manifested my operation, this is thinking from the desire as if it had already happened.

Another very useful technique of Neville's is remembering when, using this technique is a very effective way to get you into the state of thinking from the desire as if it has already happened. You can use this all day as well as when you are doing your sessions to imagine your desires.

When I was working in a job I did not particularly enjoy I used I remember when in my inner conversations to suggest that I was no longer working in that job. When I was driving to this job, which was almost an hours commute away I would say in my head over and over I remember when I had to drive that busy road for almost an hour to get to work, I am so glad that's in the past and I no longer have to drive that distance, its great being able to work from home now, and I would feel contentment and relief. I did the same on my drive home. It is like looking back on your past experience which has now been replaced by something better; this is thinking from what you desire and not thinking of it. I did this every day I went to work for over three months, before it objectified itself in my World. I didn't give up after a few weeks because nothing had changed. I persisted for over three months and then all of a sudden my "I remember when inner conversation" became my reality.

You can also use this when you go into your sleepy state and are imagining your scene that suggests your desires are a reality. Let's say you are desiring a vacation in an exotic location, as you are imagining yourself laying on your sun lounger, sipping your cocktail, looking out at the clear blue ocean and feeling the sun on your face, you can look back still in this scene in your imagination and picture yourself lying in your bed as you were imagining this scene, see the memory picture of it, and say to yourself I remember when I was once just lying in my bed, imagining this very scene and now I am here, lying on this sun lounger sipping my cocktail. Then return your attention back to your imaginative scene and feel the contentment and joy in that. By doing this you have successfully sown the seed in your imagination and your desired trip will come into your reality. You are now thinking FROM your desire and not OF your desire.

Neville Goddard's teachings work, and they are actually very simple, we just tend to complicate the process. Know what you want, construct a scene that you believe you would encounter following the accomplishment of your desire. Identify the feeling that would be yours if it had already happened, get into a sleepy relaxed state and play the scene over and over again until you get the feeling that satisfies. Then walk in this state throughout your waking day. Think from your desire; use all the techniques in this book to strengthen your state, also if you haven't already read my book on [inner conversations](#) which goes into much more detail on how to master those also, your success is guaranteed if you apply the knowledge and persist with it. Things might not change tomorrow, or next week, but they will change if you continue to live in the feeling of your new desired state and live in the end, always thinking from your desire.

Manifesting with ease is achievable, we do it every single day of our lives, but it is mainly done unconsciously, so when we meet our harvest in our outer world, we do not recognize it and wonder why such things keep happening to us. Take control of your imagination and your inner state, so that you know exactly what you are sowing in your mind and what you can expect to meet in your future as events and experiences. Never accept as final anything that you do not wish to see in your world.

Thank You

Thank you so much for taking the time to purchase and read this book. I really do hope that you have gained insights and clarity on the teachings of Neville and in the successful application of using your imagination to make your dreams a reality. If you have enjoyed or have gained anything from this book, or if you have any suggestions or points regarding the content, please take a minute to leave a review on Amazon. I read all reviews and any feedback is very much appreciated.

We are all capable of achieving our desires, as Neville said often we must be persistent and we must apply what we learn. Knowledge without action is just knowledge, if we apply what we have learned then we will experience the truth and through experience we will gain confidence in our own wonderful human imagination!

This book is small as I believe that the information can be given in a clear short way, without the added unnecessary fluffing out for length. I find this can sometimes be off putting. These techniques are simple but powerful and I know through my own experience that they work.

If you have any questions or comments for me I can be reached at ritafaithauthor@gmail.com

Until next time… Dream better than the best you know.

Printed in Great Britain
by Amazon